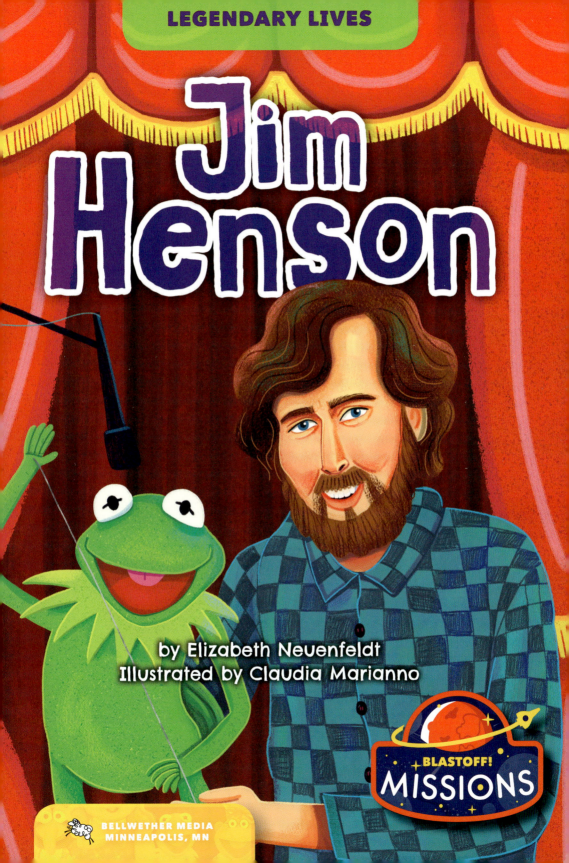

Blastoff! Missions takes you on a learning adventure! Colorful illustrations and exciting narratives highlight cool facts about our world and beyond. Read the mission goals and follow the narrative to gain knowledge, build reading skills, and have fun!

Traditional Nonfiction

Narrative Nonfiction

Blastoff! Universe

MISSION GOALS

> FIND YOUR SIGHT WORDS IN THE BOOK.

> LEARN ABOUT JIM HENSON'S LIFE.

> LEARN HOW JIM HENSON ACHIEVED HIS DREAM OF WORKING IN TELEVISION.

This edition first published in 2026 by Bellwether Media, Inc.

No part of this publication may be reproduced in whole or in part without written permission of the publisher. For information regarding permission, write to Bellwether Media, Inc., Attention: Permissions Department, 3500 American Blvd W, Suite 150, Bloomington, MN 55431.

Library of Congress Cataloging-in-Publication Data

Names: Neuenfeldt, Elizabeth author. | Marianno, Claudia illustrator.
Title: Jim Henson / by Elizabeth Neuenfeldt ; [illustrated by] Claudia Marianno.
Description: Blastoff! missions. | Minneapolis : Bellwether Media, Inc, 2025. | Series: Legendary lives | Includes bibliographical references and index. | Audience: Ages 5-8 | Audience: Grades 2-3 | Summary: "Vibrant illustrations accompany information about Jim Henson. The narrative nonfiction text is intended for students in kindergarten through third grade." -Provided by publisher Provided by publisher.
Identifiers: LCCN 2025018591 (print) | LCCN 2025018592 (ebook) | ISBN 9798893045345 library binding | ISBN 9798893047516 paperback | ISBN 9798893046724 ebook
Subjects: LCSH: Henson, Jim--Juvenile literature | Puppeteers--United States--Biography--Juvenile literature | Television producers and directors--United States--Biography--Juvenile literature | LCGFT: Biographies
Classification: LCC PN1982.H46 N49 2026 (print) | LCC PN1982.H46 (ebook) | DDC 791.5/3092--dc23/eng/20250417
LC record available at https://lccn.loc.gov/2025018591
LC ebook record available at https://lccn.loc.gov/2025018592

Text copyright © 2026 by Bellwether Media, Inc. BLASTOFF! MISSIONS and associated logos are trademarks and/or registered trademarks of Bellwether Media, Inc. Bellwether Media is a division of FlutterBee Education Group.

Editor: Rebecca Sabelko   Designer: Andrea Schneider

Printed in the United States of America, North Mankato, MN.

This is **Blastoff Jimmy**! He is here to help you on your mission and share fun facts along the way!

Table of Contents

Meet Jim Henson	4
An Early Start	6
Making the Muppets	10
Gone Too Soon	20
Glossary	22
To Learn More	23
Beyond the Mission	24
Index	24

Meet Jim Henson

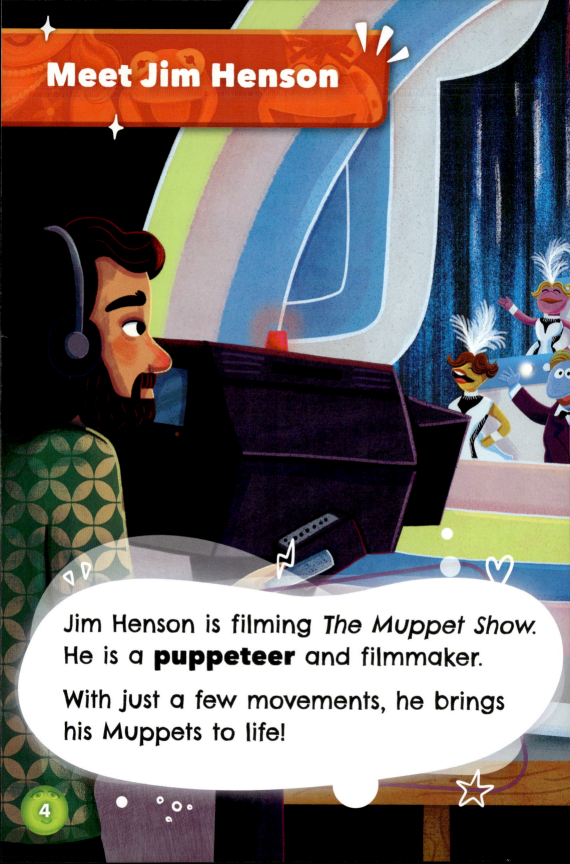

Jim Henson is filming *The Muppet Show*. He is a **puppeteer** and filmmaker.

With just a few movements, he brings his Muppets to life!

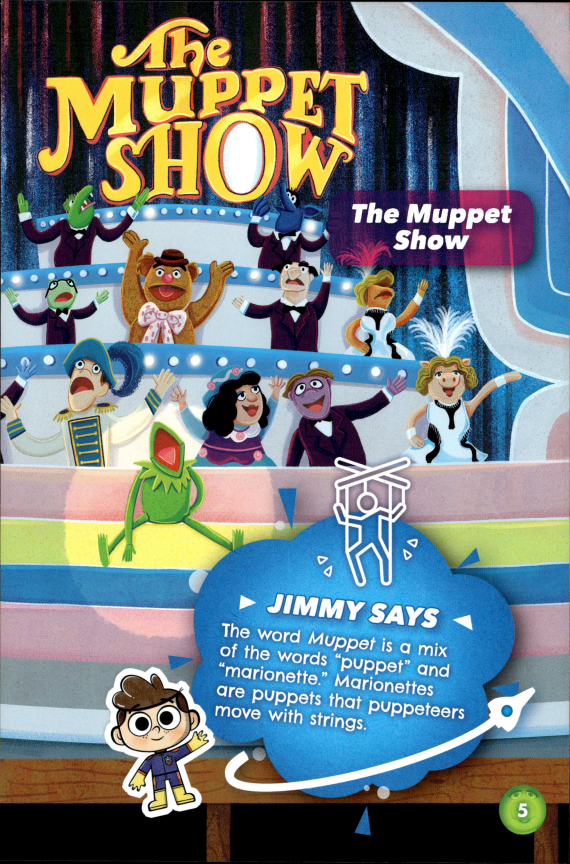

The Muppet Show

> ▶ **JIMMY SAYS** ◀
>
> The word *Muppet* is a mix of the words "puppet" and "marionette." Marionettes are puppets that puppeteers move with strings.

An Early Start

It is the 1940s. Young Jim spends time with his grandma.

She teaches Jim how to draw and sew. She **encourages** Jim to be **creative**.

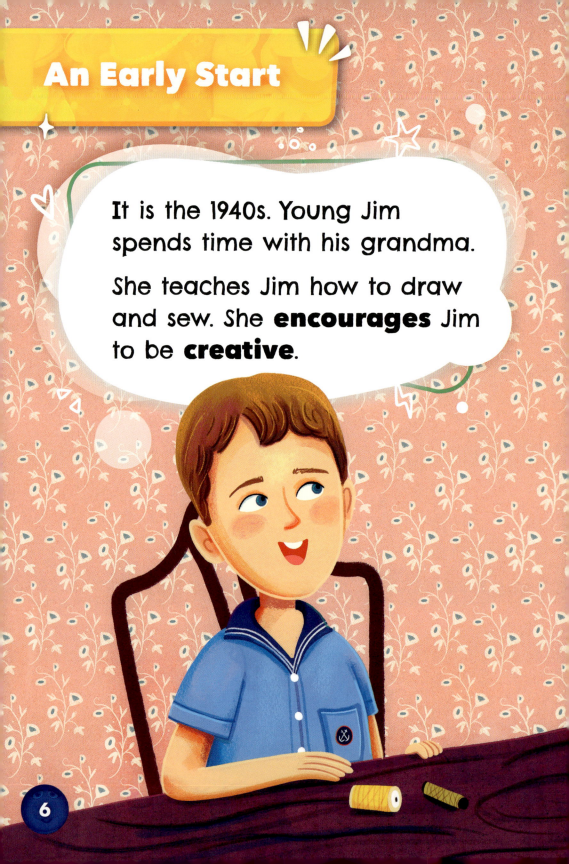

Jim is a teenager. He dreams of working in television.

A local **station** wants young puppeteers. Jim does not know much about puppets. But he gets the job!

Making the Muppets

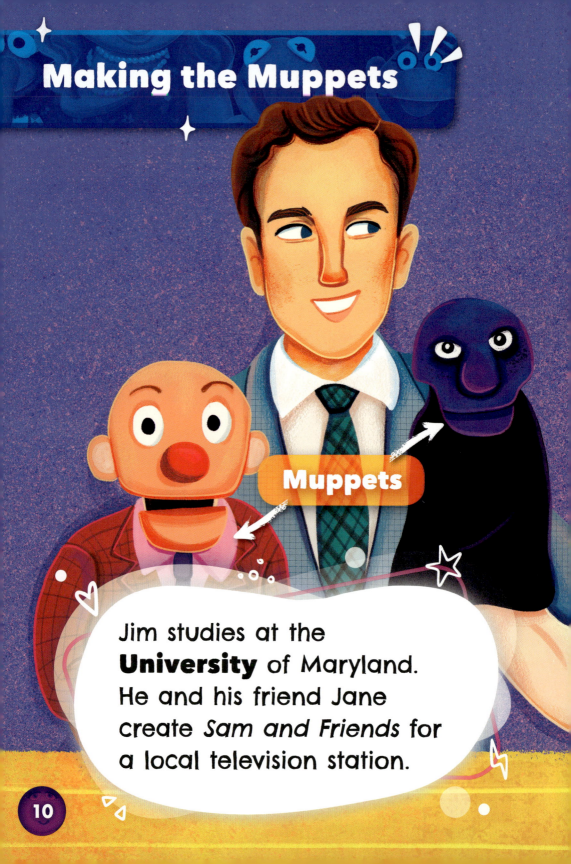

Muppets

Jim studies at the **University** of Maryland. He and his friend Jane create *Sam and Friends* for a local television station.

The show stars Jim's Muppets!

Jane

▶ **JIMMY SAYS** ◀

Jim and Jane got married in 1959. They raised five children together.

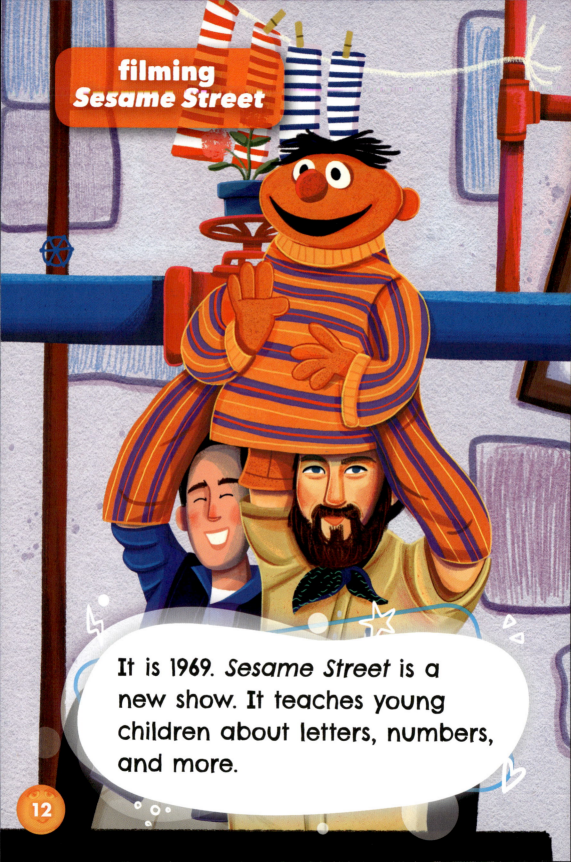

filming Sesame Street

It is 1969. *Sesame Street* is a new show. It teaches young children about letters, numbers, and more.

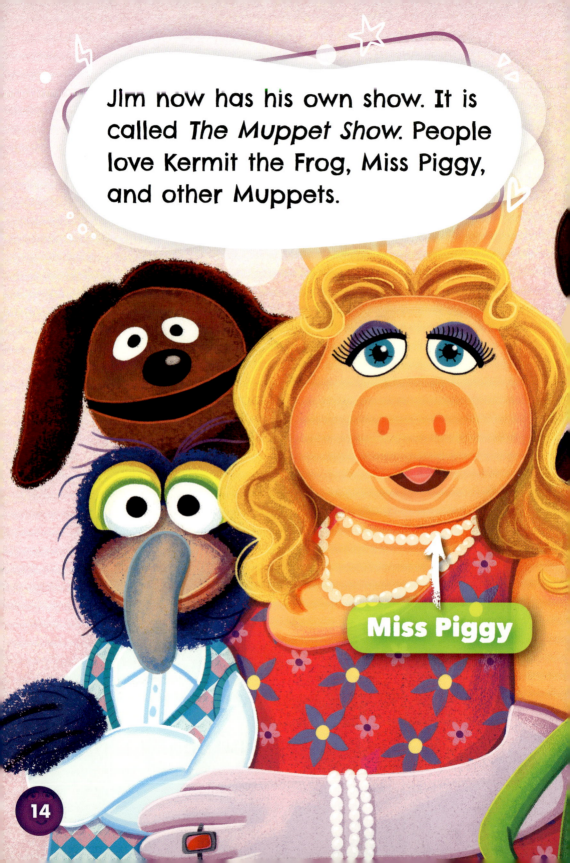

Jim now has his own show. It is called *The Muppet Show*. People love Kermit the Frog, Miss Piggy, and other Muppets.

Miss Piggy

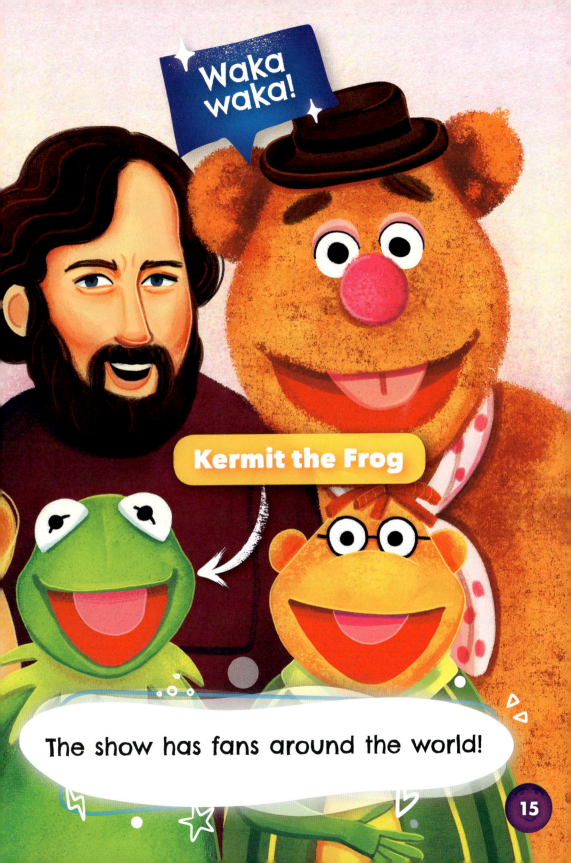

filming *The Muppet Movie*

Soon, he will start working on *Labyrinth*. Both movies are **praised** for their puppetry.

filming *The Dark Crystal*

Gone Too Soon

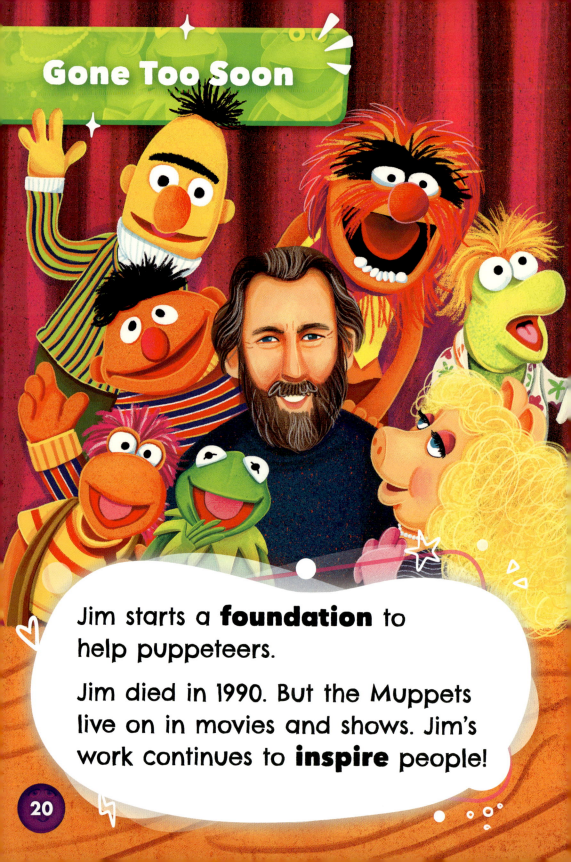

Jim starts a **foundation** to help puppeteers.

Jim died in 1990. But the Muppets live on in movies and shows. Jim's work continues to **inspire** people!

Jim Henson Profile

Born: September 24, 1936, in Greenville, Mississippi

Died: May 16, 1990

Accomplishments: Filmmaker and puppeteer known for creating the Muppets

Timeline

1954: Jim gets his first job working as a puppeteer on the *Junior Morning Show* at WTOP/CBS in Washington, D.C.

1955 to 1961: *Sam and Friends* airs on WRC TV in Washington, D.C.

1969: *Sesame Street* airs its first episode

1976: *The Muppet Show* airs its first episode

1982: *The Dark Crystal* hits theaters

Glossary

creative–able to make new or different things

directed–led people who are making a movie or show

encourages–gives the help needed to accomplish a goal

foundation–a group that gives money in order to do something that helps society

inspire–to give someone an idea about what to do or create

praised–showed approval of something

puppeteer–a person who works with puppets

station–a place where radio or television shows are made

university–a school that people go to after high school

To Learn More

AT THE LIBRARY

Hansen, Grace. *Jim Henson: Master Muppets Puppeteer & Filmmaker*. Minneapolis, Minn.: Abdo Kids, 2020.

Neuenfeldt, Elizabeth. *LeVar Burton*. Minneapolis, Minn.: Bellwether Media, 2026.

Schwartz, Heather E. *The Muppet Movie: An Official Picture Book*. Philadelphia, Pa.: Running Kids Press, 2025.

ON THE WEB

FACTSURFER

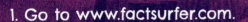

Factsurfer.com gives you a safe, fun way to find more information.

1. Go to www.factsurfer.com.

2. Enter "Jim Henson" into the search box and click 🔍.

3. Select your book cover to see a list of related content.

BEYOND THE MISSION

> WHAT FACT FROM THE BOOK DO YOU THINK WAS THE MOST INTERESTING?

> THINK ABOUT A PERSON WHO INSPIRES YOU. WHAT DO THEY INSPIRE YOU TO ACHIEVE?

> THINK ABOUT CREATING YOUR OWN PUPPET. DRAW A DESIGN FOR IT.

Index

Dark Crystal, The, 18, 19
directed, 18
draw, 6
dreams, 8
fans, 15
filmmaker, 4
foundation, 20
grandma, 6
Jane, 10, 11
Kermit the Frog, 14, 15
Labyrinth, 19
Miss Piggy, 14
Muppet Movie, The, 16, 17

Muppet Show, The, 4, 5, 14, 15
Muppets, 4, 5, 11, 13, 14, 15, 17, 20
profile, 21
puppeteer, 4, 5, 8, 19, 20
Sam and Friends, 10, 11
Sesame Street, 12, 13
sew, 6, 7
television, 8, 10, 13
University of Maryland, 10